Business Growth Secrets

Book 1
SECRETS TO LONG-TERM SALES GROWTH

By
Dr. John A. Weber
University of Notre Dame

Book 1 of 8 in the
Business Growth Secrets Book Series

Reactions to the Business Growth Series Book Series

Become the next sales superstar in your company! Blow away your sales targets. Be your boss's 'go to' sales pro. See some of the hundreds of 5* reviews below - from sales pros who have successfully started or totally relaunched their careers using this innovative, proven selling process.

What sales professionals are saying about the Business Growth Secrets book series

Essential Reading for Sales Professionals

- **A must-have for marketing & sales professionals.** "This book series is as well-organized as it is insightful. Crucial information is integrated and neatly packed into brief sections that capture one's attention with clear examples, observations and caveats. Professionals in any field can benefit from this book series, but for marketing/sales professionals this book series is a must-have!"
  Greg G.
- **A treasure trove of great information.** "I've been finding a treasure trove of GREAT information in these books. I feel like I'm getting a business degree in selling just by reading these books."
  David L.
- **This book series has turned around my sales career!** "These books have become my 'how-to' guide – literally turning around my sales career. The process explained has been particularly helpful when I'm pursuing big ticket sales opportunities."
  M. Murphy
- **My 'go-to-source' for selling success.** "Having recently embarked on a career in sales, I can say unequivocally that the detailed approach presented so clearly in this book series has been a difference maker for me for both preparing for my interviews and now as my 'go-to-source' for my selling success."
  Barbara B
- **A must read for anyone in the marketing world.** "These books are a 'must read' for anyone in the marketing world seeking new perspectives and insights for growing their sales."
  Danielle P.

Easy to Understand and Retain

- **Well-organized, easy to follow.** "These books are all well-organized and closely linked - offering a clear, concise outline at the beginning of each book, which make it easier to follow along the different stages of the selling process. A great read for anyone wanting to learn to sell more effectively!"
  Sofia S.
- **Short chapters.** The short chapters make it easy to pay attention, as they break down the information into specific smaller steps. This helps to understand, rather than be overwhelmed by the logical selling process presented."
  Jane E.
- **Bring the selling process to life.** "Whereas most sales books get bogged down with verbose conceptual descriptions, the books in this series bring to life the selling process in a simple, engaging manner – highly recommended for any veteran or aspiring sales professional."
  Jeff A.
- **A quick read, easily digestible.** "The books in this series are a quick read and are easily digestible for anyone looking to improve their selling skills – whether new to sales or a professional sales veteran."
  Mark C.

A Logical Process

- **A logical checklist for planning any selling effort.** "This book series provides a clear and thorough 10-step process on how to tackle and close any prospective sale."
  J. Agar
- **Clear structure and supporting diagrams.** "The selling process detailed in these books is ideal for anyone favoring clear, unambiguous structure presented with easy-to-understand supporting diagrams and examples."
  A.C
- **An integrated approach.** "Rather than presenting a bunch of theories and terms scattered about overwhelmingly long chapters, these books present a logical, integrated approach - neatly packed in brief chapters that use clear examples throughout to capture and hold one's attention."
  G. Garner.
- **Clearly laid out tools – for immediately use.** "I cannot say enough good things about this book series. The books provide a

clear, proven way for successful selling -- full of easy-to-use tools one can use immediately in the real world to enhance sales!"
    T. Redman

A Fun Read, Full of Real World Examples

- **Fun and engaging.** "What a refreshing change from the typical book about selling! Reading these books was fun and engaging, as they include tons of pictures, cartoons, amusing characters, and insightful charts and exhibits."
  Darin C.
- **Very enjoyable reading.** "I never thought I'd actually enjoy learning about sales. But these books have totally changed my opinion. They make the whole selling process come alive with cogent, often times humorous characters, dialog and examples."
  Adam S.
- **The books are a joy to read.** "The Business Growth Secrets books are a real joy to read, as they are not only super-logical, but also filled with straightforward clarifying illustrations, humorous characters and anecdotes, and extensive dialogues clarifying key points."
  E. Reilly

Business Growth Secrets Book Series

Book 1: Secrets to Long Term Sales Growth

Book 2: Secrets to Planning Sales Growth

Book 3: Secrets to Preparing for Sales Growth, Part 1

Book 4: Secrets to Preparing for Sales Growth, Part 2

Book 5: *Secrets to Making the Sale, Part 1*

Book 6: *Secrets to Making the Sale, Part 2*

Book 7: Secrets to Negotiating, Closing & Implementation

Book 8: Secrets to Ensuring Continuous Sales Growth

Copyright © 2022 by John A. Weber.

All rights reserved. No part of this publication may be reproduced, distributed or transmitted in any form or by any means, including photocopying, recording, or other electronic or mechanical methods, without the prior written permission of the publisher, except in the case of brief quotations embodied in critical reviews and certain other noncommercial uses permitted by copyright law. For permission requests, write to the publisher, addressed "Attention: Permissions Coordinator," at the address below.

Dr. John A. Weber (weber,1@nd.edu)
Mendoza College of Business
Notre Dame, IN 46560
www.linkedin.com/in/johnweberphd/

Book Layout ©2022 BookDesignTemplates.com

Business Growth Secrets: Book 1 (of 8) – Secrets to Long-term Sales Growth / Dr. John A. Weber —1st ed.
ISBN: 9798637593194

Introduction

The Business Growth Secrets Book Series is written to help companies realize continuous, aggressive sales and profit growth. *All materials presented in these books have been tested countless times through the author's own growth planning consulting experiences with scores of major firms.* (See Author profile, next.)

Each book in the series is fast-moving and easy to read, featuring short, single-concept chapters, accompanied by many cartoons that bring to life the principles as they are presented. To build and maintain interest, the various concepts and processes detailed in the book series are presented in actual Account Marketing scenarios that include a cast of fun characters introduced and followed along the way, providing a lively and entertaining storyline.

The series starts (**Books 1-4**) with concepts, frameworks and practical planning perspectives that together provide the base necessary for any firm desiring to get on a consistent growth path.

The series then moves on (**Books 5-6**) to pursue the commonsense notion that sales and profit growth are achieved one profitable sale at a time. Here enters Solution Selling® - an ultra-effective selling system used for training more than a million sales professionals in large and small companies around the globe. The books in this section provide a hands-on review of all the details of the Solution Selling® process, with the author's own interpretation and extensions.

The final books in the series (**Books 7-8**) overlay the selling processes covered in the earlier books in the series with negotiating principles and a sales management system that enable the conversion of one profitable sale at a time into consistent, aggressive, long-term sales and profit growth.

Combining the planning perspectives clearly laid out in the early books in the series with the detailed selling process and sales management system outlined in the latter books ultimately yields an effective, proven formula for achieving the goal of continuous growth of sales and profits.

About the Author

John A. Weber (Ph.D., University of Wisconsin), is Emeritus Professor of Marketing at the University of Notre Dame where he taught for decades, only recently retiring. He has published over seventy articles, monographs, books, and computers programs on planning corporate growth.

John has worked with hundreds of major firms - among them more than thirty Fortune 500 companies - helping them to identify and pursue new sales and profit growth opportunities. Corporate clients have included General Electric, AT&T, IBM, 3M, Xerox, Bristol-Myers, International Paper, Bell South, Miles Labs, Pioneer Seed, Honeywell, Mastic, Nekoosa, Bradley, Thomaston Mills, Kellogg, Certainteed, Uniroyal, Whirlpool, American Greetings, Square D, Cabot, Richards Medical, Continental Can (JSC/CCA), Camshaft Machine, Adria Labs, Jeld-Wen, Dukane, Gould, Hammermill, Sears, Federal Express, and many other companies manufacturing and marketing a wide range of industrial and consumer products and services.

Professor Weber is a certified instructor of Solution Selling®. In addition to his own extensive material on planning corporate growth, the Business Growth Secrets Book Series integrates his interpretation & expansion of the Solution Selling® system - with SPI's approval, but without SPI's carte blanche endorsement of all the specifics of his professional interpretation and expansion.

Acknowledgements

All the young professionals shown and listed below made significant contributions to the development, drafting, and editing of this work. Thank you all!

Back: *Colleen MacDonald, John Weber, Collin Erker, Phil Anderson, Sam Dettman, Will Ivancic, Ozzy Rocha, Chris Jacques, Rob Kirk, Eric Chyriwski, Erin Laughlin.* Middle: *Chris Davis, Amanda Walter, Kate Albertini, Morgan Walsh, Katie Adams, Maya Pillai,* Front: *Alejandra Barrios, Teresa Keeney, Alexa Wilson.*

Special acknowledgement to ***Alyx Weber and Jack Clarke*** for their help with proofing and particularly to the enthusiastic individuals shown below for their extraordinary dedication and contributions. Thank you!

Catherine Russell, Michael Nokes, Mike Donnelly, Leo Dipiero, Laura Taylor, Kate Albertini, Chris Jacques, Kristina Hamilton, Kirsten Bescher, Elizabeth Linnemanstons

Business Growth Secrets

Book 1
SECRETS TO LONG-TERM SALES GROWTH

Contents Summary

Importance of Growth
    1. Growth is King!

Why is Steady Growth so Difficult to Achieve?
    2. What Business Are You Really In?
    3. You Need the Best Overall Solution Value
    4. You Cannot Stop Commodity Drift

Requirements for Steady, Profitable Growth
    5. Marketing Strategies to Counter Commodity Drift
    6. Focus on Value
    7. Importance of Adding Sustainable Advantages
    8. Beware of Pricing Traps
    9. Know Your Customers, Competition & Solution
    10. Importance of Leadership & Teamwork

A 'Master Selling Approach' Drives Growth
    11. A 'Master Selling Approach' Drives Growth

Contents Details

1. Growth is King 1
   - The 'Envelope Method' 2
   - Steady Top Line Revenue Growth is Key! 3
   - Growing Companies Are 'Happy' Companies 4
   - Grow or Go 5
   - Can Your Company Achieve Steady Top Line Growth? Yes 6
2. What Business Are You Really In? 7
   - Try This 9
   - Visionary Exercise 12
3. You Need the Best *OVERALL* Market Solution 13
   - Social Media's Role in Enhancing Market Solutions 16
   - Online Surveys. 17
4. You Cannot Stop Commodity Drift 19
   - You Cannot Stop Commodity Drift 19
   - What is 'Commodity Drift?' 20
   - Why Is Commodity Drift So Inevitable? 21
   - Social Media Can Accelerates or Slow Commodity Drift 23
5. Common Sense Strategies to Counter Commodity Drift 25
   - Pro-Active Marketing Strategies to Delay Commodity Drift .25
   - Re-Active Strategies to Counter Current Commodity Drift 28
6. Focus on Value 31
   - What is Value & What Do Our Target Customers Value? 32
   - The Lessons of This Scenario 33
7. Importance of Sustainable Advantages (Differentiators) 35
   - Consider Another Example. 35
   - The Lessons of This Scenario 37

What New Features & Services Should a Company Add to Stimulate Growth without Compromising Profits? 37

Potential Sources of Sustainability 38

The Bottom Line on Sustainability 39

8. Beware of Pricing Traps 41
Image as a Sustainable Differentiator: The Price Umbrella ... 41

The Industry Leader Should Provide a Price Umbrella 42

Reaction Threshold 43

The Lesson 44

9. Know Your Customers, Competitors & Your Market Solution 45

Know Your Customers and Competitors 45

How the Internet and Social Media have Changed the Game 46

Know Your *Overall* Market Solution 46

10. Importance of Leadership and Teamwork 49
Leadership and Teamwork 49

What Does It Take to be a Sales Superstar? 50

Who's He? 50

Star 'Rainmakers' Are Made, Not Born 51

Sales Superstars Leverage Social Media 53

11. A 'Master Selling Approach' Drives Growth 55
What's the Secret? 56

A 'Master Selling Approach' Drives the Growth Plan 56

Sales Team Benefits from Using a Single Selling Approach ... 58

Sales Management Benefits from a Single Selling Approach. 58

Now, What's Next? 60

CHAPTER 1

Growth is King

"Fat, drunk and stupid is no way to go through life, son." This sound observation came from Dean Wormer while chastising Flounder in the movie classic, *Animal House*.

Although Dean Wormer was referencing the crazy college life that Flounder was experiencing, a similar observation can be made in reference to the corporate world: **Constantly struggling to meet quarterly profit projections through cost cutting and massaging the numbers is no way to run a business! It's not fun either** ☹ !

The 'Envelope Method'

The envelope method consists of cashing your check each month (or week), paying all fixed monthly or weekly bills, divvying up the remaining proceeds into separate envelopes for identified, budgeted items (food, baby sitter, entertainment, automobile expenses, household maintenance, etc.) – and then pulling cash out of envelopes as expenses occur. Finally, and inevitably, as the next payday approaches, you start raiding any envelopes with money remaining in order to cover expenses where the envelopes are 'mysteriously' empty.

Years ago, our young family discovered that the 'envelope method' (See Exhibit) is no fun. By the time my wife and I were approaching thirty, with two kids and another on the way, the envelope method was getting old! Although this method worked to keep us on budget for several years, the approach just didn't cut it as our household continued to expand. When it came time to cover larger, 'unpredictable' costs such as school expenses, a larger home for our growing family, emergency automobile repairs, and the like, we realized we needed a different strategy.

Something had to give if we were to move into the future without constant worries, quick fixes, and spending squabbles. Sound familiar? How fun is that?

Happy ending. For the decades since then, we have managed to stay out of debt, putting all our children through college and maintaining a comfortable - albeit not lavish - lifestyle. What's more, we have also avoided both 'panic' money problems and the related, never-fun 'family money discussions.'

How did we do it? Simple – I was trained well enough to establish a second income stream through providing consulting services, which eventually doubled my 'day job' salary. *More income trumps cost cutting every time!*

Steady Top Line Revenue Growth is Key!

Increased revenue solves existing problems and helps avoid new ones. Not having to worry about paying the bills made our family life much less stressful and much more enjoyable! Who doesn't like that? Increased revenue enabled us to focus on opportunities ahead rather than on budget cutting and its subsequent negatives.

Well-planned revenue growth can do the same thing for a corporation as it does for a family. In fact, if there existed a list of 'magic elixirs' for corporate problems, then steady revenue growth would certainly be THE number one item on that list!

Of course, you say... but... much, much easier said than done. You bet. That's the motivation for this book and its exact purpose: to help your company achieve more regular, profitable revenue growth.

Growing Companies Are 'Happy' Companies

Few complaints are heard at companies where 'home-grown' organic revenues and profits consistently grow 5-10% per year. Outside players such as stockholders, distributors, and suppliers are pleased, as are insiders, ranging from C-level players (e.g., CEO, CFO, COO, CMO, etc.) to operating players (like those involved in supply chain management, manufacturing, finance, and marketing).

Instead of trouble-shooting the problems associated with a lack of foresight, vision, and planning, these companies can devote much more time to finding and pursuing new, creative growth opportunities.

Grow or Go

One insightful study[1] uncovered a very interesting phenomenon: the expected tenure of a new Chief Marketing Officer (CMO) is less than half that of a newly minted CEO (23 months vs. 54 months). Why do CMOs get fired so often? Usually it is due to faltering top line revenue growth. For, without top line growth, the bottom line inevitably fades, resulting in pressures to blame someone. The most obvious and likely scapegoat is the officer in charge of revenue growth, that is, the CMO. Thus, the key to a long and successful tenure as a Marketing Executive is to keep top line revenue growing – year after year after year!

Can Your Company Achieve Steady Top Line Revenue Growth? Sure, You Can!

Certainly, steady growth is easier said than done in today's increasingly competitive environment. The truism 'nothing worthwhile is easy' seems appropriate. But fear not - steady growth is possible. The first step to achieving regular growth is to recognize the reasons why so many companies fail to meet the growth challenge. In the following chapters, we discuss the primary causes of faltering revenue growth. We will then provide practical perspectives and tools for successfully addressing the challenge of achieving steady and profitable top line growth.

***

In the next several chapters we discuss the hurdles that inhibit steady, profitable growth in today's markets. *Then we move on to the important stuff – "How to Grow Consistently & Profitably!"*

CHAPTER 2

What Business Are You Really In?

In this chapter, we will begin the discussion of why steady, profitable growth is so difficult to achieve in today's markets.

Growth starts when you first recognize your company's true business. You can do this by asking what set of fundamental needs your company is trying to address with its current primary product or service. Focus on identifying those underlying needs. Thinking of your business as providing solutions rather than specific products or services can open entirely new avenues of potential growth.

You already know your customers and their needs related to your current products and services. Who better than you to seek out new product and service areas that more adequately satisfy those needs? If you don't, your competitors will – taking away your customers, your sales, and your growth.

Brick & Mortar Book Stores Example

Take Blockbuster for example. Blockbuster was late in recognizing the industry trend towards video streaming. Netflix CEO and co-founder Reed Hastings approached Blockbuster CEO John Antioco in 2011 seeking a partnership between the two rental services, but Antioco declined. You can thank Blockbuster's short-sightedness for your new neighborhood eyesore. Michael Brush of MSN Money observes that "Video rental icon Blockbuster is a great example of how technological change can crush winners that fail to keep up. First, Blockbuster got hammered as video rentals began moving to mail distribution pioneered by Netflix. ... Now, video distribution is shifting to the Internet, and Blockbuster is lagging again. The amount of content you can download directly will make Blockbuster obsolete." Building off that sentiment, Strata Capital's Scott Stevens states "It seems to me, though, that technology has doomed Blockbuster as we know it. But at least we can all say goodbye to late fees forever."[2]

Like Blockbuster, Borders was also a victim of technological change. So, what went wrong for Borders? First came the Internet, which brought aggressive price competition from Amazon.com. Then, Wal-Mart's tendency to slash prices on bestsellers and Amazon's ability to match those price cuts made competition even worse for Borders. Now, Amazon's Kindle and other e-book readers are gaining popularity. More and more readers simply download digital books at much lower prices than print versions. All these trends reduced the need for a brick-and-mortar bookstore like Borders, which filed for bankruptcy because of their high inventory and store-related costs.[3]

Stand-Alone GPS Units Example

Magellan, the former leader in GPS, represents another once-great company that was doomed. GPS, the technology that plots your location via satellite, served as Magellan's relatively unique advantage for years, but soon became available just about everywhere. Besides dashboard GPS devices in cars, consumers could soon access GPS services on their smart-phones & cameras. This was a natural progression in technology. In due time, consumers had few reasons to buy stand-alone GPS devices from Magellan because software on their phone performs an identical service.

To better understand how GPS was increasingly commoditized, consider the intense price competition in this category. On Black Friday in 2011, vendors like Magellan were offering generic GPS devices as low as $69. This price was $21 below the cost of materials in each device, but Magellan offered such a low price in order to try to maintain their current shelf space. You know a business appears doomed when it has to sell below costs, even temporarily, just to stay in the game.[4]

Try This

Here's an exercise in discovering new growth opportunities. Consider the multiple "Current Products or Services" listed in Column 1 of the upcoming exhibit. Ask yourself, what fundamental, underlying need is each product or service providing? For example, Column 3 suggests some options or possibilities for identifying 'what business' the listed companies are actually in. Column 4 asks the question: what new 'solutions' might be the future for that industry? To succeed, a company must understand who their real competitors are - today and in years ahead. The company that does this the best typically wins the game. Those who lack foresight and fail to adapt will lose out. **_What is your company's primary product or service? What business is your company actually in?_** Consider these examples. Focus on Exhibit, Columns 3 & 4.

1 Current Product or Service	2 Company Examples	3 What Business Are You Really In?	4 Potential Products or Services to Consider?
Automobile leasing	Wheels, Corporate Fleet Services, Enterprise	Convenient, economical transportation business	Short-term car rental (i.e. Zipcar)
Bookstores	Barnes & Noble, Books-A-Million, Borders, B. Dalton	Personal leisure and education	E-commerce bookstore and Kindles
Computer aided design software	Autodesk, Avid Technology, ANSYS	Virtual product and building design	Software configuration management software
Computer hard-drives	Seagate, IBM, Fujitsu, Hitachi, Maxtor	Information storage business	Data storage in the cloud
Copiers	Xerox, Canon, Toshiba	Document management business	Document management software & Data Integration
ERP Systems	Best Software, Sage, Microsoft, Oracle	Company management & control business	CRM software
Fragrances	Sentient, CPL Aromas, Quest Int'l, International Flavors &	Business of making the human body, animals, objects or living	Longer lasting, dynamic fragrances. Substitutes for
Fractional Airline Service	NetJets, Marquis Jets, Flexjet, Avant Air	Travel convenience business	C2C Internet Service that matches renters and lenders
Newspaper media	NY Times, Tribune Company, Washington Post	Information delivery business	Online news media
Office furniture	Steelcase, Inscape, Commercial Furniture Group	Office design & productivity	Interior design
Office leasing	Intelligent Office, Regus, Your Office Management	Office reach and productivity	Short-term office rental
Relocation companies	Cort	Relocation services	Relocation software (analyzes and compares potential new
Retail self checkout Machines	Fujitsu (U-Scan), IBM, NCR, Pan-Oston,	Retail productivity services	Digital touch-and-go payment services
Radio Frequency Identification systems (RFID)	Texas Instruments, Sun Microsystems, HP, MIT	Manufacturing, Inventory & Distribution productivity	More advanced ID technologies – e.g., Micro-sizing sensors
Sales Force Automation Systems	Salesforce.com, Sage (Sales Logix), Oracle (Siebel CRM)	Sales force productivity	Project management software
Security Services	ADT, Bosch Security Systems, Protection One	Safety & Loss prevention services	More automated & sensitive security systems
Signs	Daktronics, Lamar, 3M Digital Signage, LSI Industries	Visual communications / promotion	Digital signage
Supply chain management systems	Sirva, UPS, Federal Express, Kronos, IBM	Increasing the efficiency & productivity of Inbound &	Private US Postal Service
Temporary Help	Manpower, Kelly, Insperity	Human resource services	Recruiting software
Tracking technology	Garmin, Hewlett-Packard, Trimble Navigation	Location & Navigation efficiency & productivity	Retail location analysis

What is your company's primary product or service? What business is your company actually in? Consider these examples. Focus on Columns 3 & 4 of the Exhibit.

SECRETS TO LONG-TERM SALES GROWTH 11

What is your company's primary product or service? What business is your company actually in? Consider these examples. Focus on Columns 3 & 4 of the Exhibit.

1 Current Product or Service	2 Company Examples	3 What Business Are You Really In?	4 Potential Products or Services to Consider?
Translation services	L-3 Communications, Lionbridge Technologies, SDL International	Global communications productivity	Real-time Automated translation software
Travel Agency	American Express, Travelocity, Expedia, American Automobile Assn	Travel management services + related substitutes & complements	Go to Meeting
Uniforms	Cintas, Unifirst, Superior Uniform Group	Better look, higher efficiency & productivity of uniform related	Cross-company imaging
Web-Analytics	Google Analytics, Omniture, Coremetrics, Visistat	Helping customers develop and execute more efficient and productive web promotions	Social media
Web-based Meetings	Web-Ex, Go to Meeting	Improving efficiency & productivity of meetings	Virtual Office?
Web-based phone service	Vonage, Phone power, ViaTalk, ITP, Lingo	More efficient audio communication	other web-based communications services

Growth Starts with Discovering What Business You Are Really In!

Visionary Exercise

Pull up this YouTube video called "A Day Made of Glass" by Corning "Glass" – or is it "Glass?"
http://www.youtube.com/watch_popup?v=6Cf7IL_eZ38&vq=medium; then https://www.mandatory.com/living/945283-cornings-day-made-glass-finally-became-reality

Watch this video.

Now, ask yourself, what business is Corning Glass in?

Then use that visionary perspective to ask yourself, **what business is your company in?**

CHAPTER 3

You Need the Best *OVERALL* Market Solution

In this chapter, we continue to discuss the important reasons why steady, profitable growth is so difficult to achieve in today's markets.

Firms' failure to explicitly recognize that they are each selling a 'total market solution' rather than a specific product or service often leads to constant struggles in trying to achieve steady, profitable growth. This chapter emphasizes that the company with the best solution will grow most steadily over the long-term.

This notion that 'you need the best solution' is not as obvious as it may seem. To start, what do we mean by the 'best solution?' The best solution is *the solution that has the highest overall net value for the target customer*. Several concepts make up that statement.

First, when we talk of the 'best solution,' we are talking about much more than the 'core' or 'naked' solution. We are talking about the *overall* solution. A company's overall market solution includes a core product or service surrounded by a whole bundle of potential auxiliary attributes and related benefits. A wide range of attributes might be relevant – for example, cutting-edge technology, superior customer service, data integration, support services for the customer, etc. Consider the examples in the expanded exhibit entitled "Flexible Market Solution".[5] These examples illustrate just a few of the many potential ways to enhance a core solution. The enhancements that are most valued and appropriate will vary by target customer segment and from one customer to the next.

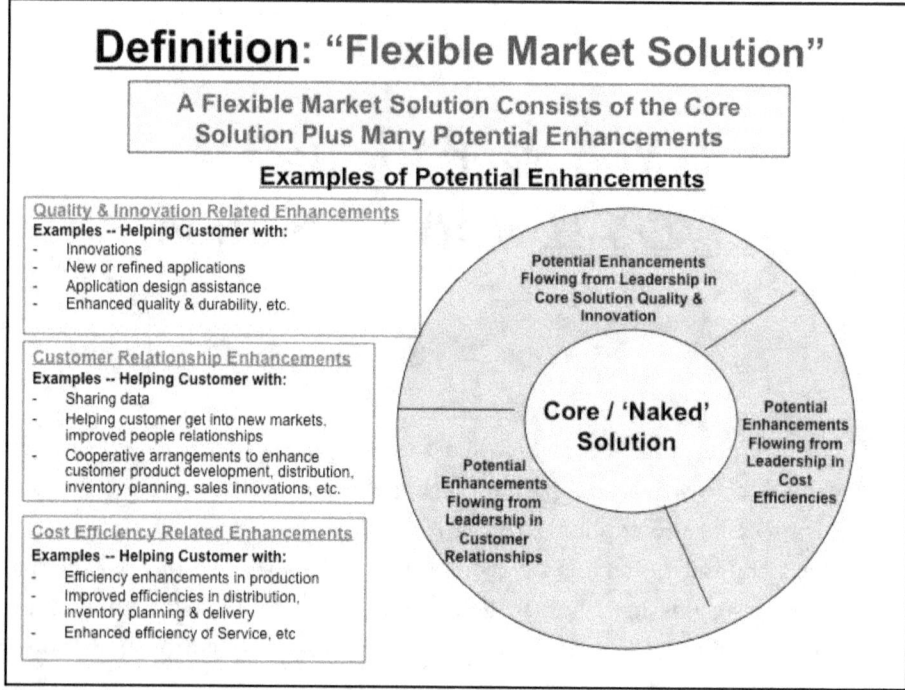

A company's overall solution does not have to be 'perfect' in order to be the best overall solution in the industry. It just has to be better than the primary competitor's overall solution.

Why is this the case? How can a company with an adequate yet competitively-inferior core solution beat out a competitor that has a clearly superior core solution? The winning company simply does a better job of listening to the customer, constantly taking the target customers' pulse and regularly adjusting its overall solution to best match dynamic customer needs and expectations. Competitors that continually dump resources into improving already adequate core solutions often falter. Meanwhile, competitors that spend more resources on listening to their target customer ultimately succeed over the longer term – assuming they respond to the needs of the client by surrounding an adequate solution with specific customer-valued attributes.

SECRETS TO LONG-TERM SALES GROWTH

You Don't Have to Be Perfect, Just Better Than the Competition

Listen to the Customers, Not the Engineers

Social Media's Role in Enhancing Market Solutions

As markets, customer demands, and competition change more rapidly, it becomes more important each year for firms to continually seek customer input and to respond to changes in customers' wants and concerns. Through using comprehensive Social Media Programs, firms today can do just that.

These programs make it easier and more efficient to monitor and learn about customers' relevant concerns with existing market solutions and to identify what specific new features or services are desired. This information can, in turn, be immediately fed to product development, customer service, IT, or other relevant departments for their consideration - which often leads to a development of better overall market solutions. Customers can then more readily and effectively be informed of new features or corrective actions through prominent updates on the company's web-site and in one or more of the company's specialty blogs. (More on this in the *Social Media Strategies* chapter).

Online Surveys.

Today any company can use low cost or even free online survey capabilities to monitor its customer community. These surveys can engage actual and potential customers in meaningful discussions to improve the company's products and support services (i.e., overall market solutions). This easy, fast, and relatively inexpensive survey capability can also be used to generate quick and useful answers to pressing questions that a company may have regarding any actual or prospective dimension of its overall market solutions.

CHAPTER 4

You Cannot Stop Commodity Drift

In this chapter we discuss yet more reasons why steady, profitable growth is so difficult to achieve in today's markets.

You Cannot Stop Commodity Drift

Bet on this: The attractiveness of every overall market solution for every relevant segment declines over time, reflecting the inevitable drift toward commodity status - with squeezed profit margins. <u>This drift can be slowed down but cannot be stopped.</u> Therefore, in order to consistently expand sales and profits, *a company must constantly seek out new market segments for current market solutions and continuously add entirely new market solutions to its portfolio.*

What is 'Commodity Drift?'[6]

Commodity Drift is the gradual, but continuous power shift from suppliers to buyers for virtually any market solution. Initially, the market solution is an innovative, yet relatively simple core solution that can support a high price because it is unique and lacks competition. In this introductory, innovative stage, the solution requires few costly add-ons (refer back to the concept of a 'total market solution') to attract initial customers, often referred to as the 'innovator customer segment.' Thus, with high price and low costs, the profit margin is high during this introductory stage.

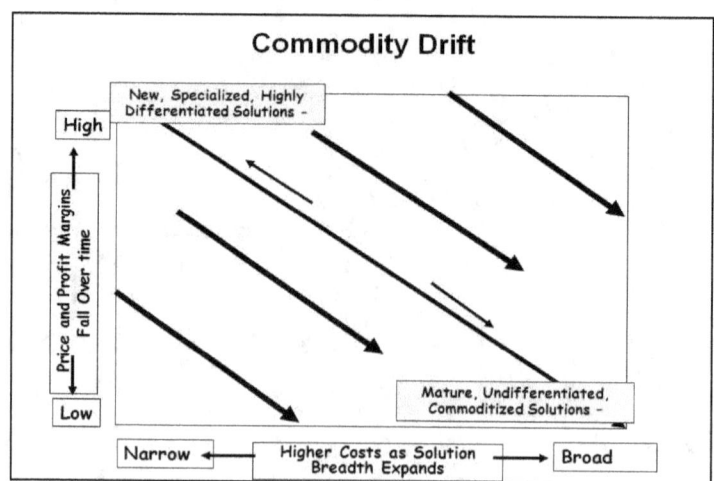

The next stage is undesirable, but inevitable. The high profit margin reaped by the original solution innovator immediately attracts competitors. These competitors gain access to the new market by offering the same fundamental core innovation at a lower price, while also often adding new features and services. The higher-cost from these additional features and services coupled with the lower price both quickly drive down profit margin for all competitors, including the original innovator. This process continues over time until the once-attractive market reaches commodity status. Commodity status is characterized by low prices, high supplier costs, and miniscule profit margins. This phenomenon is known as *Commodity Drift*. Although this profit-sapping drift may be slowed (through strategies considered in the following chapters), it is inevitable for virtually every market segment and every solution.

Why Is Commodity Drift So Inevitable?

Why Does Commodity Drift Occur?

- **Competitive Dynamics**
  - **More competitors (domestic and foreign)**
  - **More sophisticated & specialized competitors** – competitors are more carefully studying (technology enabled) & catering to narrower Customer Value Segments
  - *More Responsive & Aggressive Competitors* - improved ability (technology enabled) & willingness to respond more quickly to changing customer requirements & desires
  - As a result, **Solution Breadth Continues to Expand** (horizontal axis of Commodity Drift matrix)

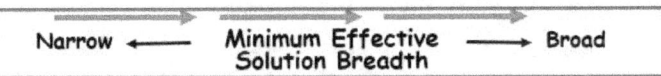

Narrow ← Minimum Effective Solution Breadth → Broad

Competitors

The high profits from innovative new solutions quickly attract global competitors. These new players enter the market using alternative approaches to try to establish themselves and capture a share of the growing market segment. Some new competitors simply lower their prices, while others maintain the current dominant price but add any number of costly frills to their product or service. Still other companies both lower price and add frills in the effort to grab market share. Inevitably, this flood of competitors drives down prices, increases costs, and causes once-high profit margins to disintegrate.

Ever-rising Customer Expectations

Rising customer expectations further accelerate Commodity Drift. Customers demand lower and lower prices and new and improved features. Naturally, these demands lead to even faster declining profit margins. More competitors and more intense competition give target customers more choices and more leverage to continually demand 'more for less.' This happens incessantly for the broad cross-section of market solutions and segments.

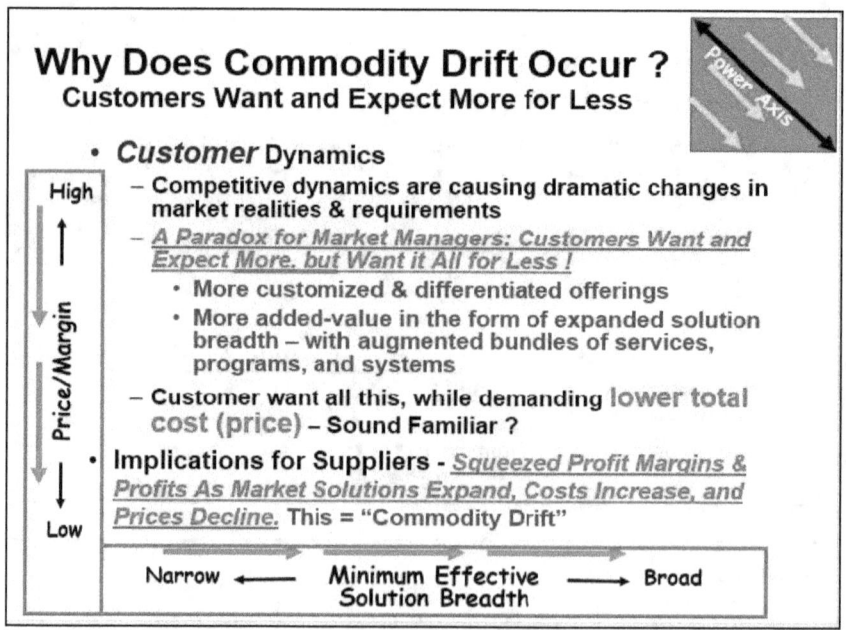

Thus, Commodity Drift causes a market shifts away from attractive, highly differentiated core solutions with high profit margins, towards lower-priced, frilled, higher cost solutions with lower-profit margins.

Social Media Accelerates Commodity Drift, but also Provides Vehicles to Help Slow the Drift

The proliferation of social media platforms and the ever-expanding use of social media are twin forces that accelerate Commodity Drift in both consumer and business-to-business markets. Actual and potential customers now have the capability to learn about new competitive offerings almost instantaneously, which enables them to pressure suppliers into matching or even surpassing their competitors' market offers or face the risk of losing out. In turn, this incredibly fast pace of competitive responses leads consumers to continue to set expectations of receiving 'more and more for less and less.'

Fortunately, sellers can also use social media to help cope with Commodity Drift. More specifically, various social media have enhanced the ways that sellers can listen to, engage, and build relationships with existing and potential customers. For example, sellers can monitor and learn what product-specific focused interest groups, blogs and white papers are saying about them and their primary brand competitors, as well as what specific new features and services actual and potential customers are demanding. This regular monitoring of social media by sellers does not slow down the Commodity Drift but can help guide strategy development toward reducing the negative impacts of the inevitable drift on the bottom line.

**

In the next chapter we consider additional potential marketing strategies to employ in order to counter Commodity Drift, *including the need to think innovatively and to regularly pursue new segments.*

CHAPTER 5

Common Sense Strategies to Counter Commodity Drift

In the previous chapters, we considered reasons why steady growth is so difficult for most firms to achieve. Now we consider some requirements for achieving steady growth – i.e., selling success. **We will cover these growth prerequisites in the next six chapters.**

In this chapter, we address two types of 'Common Sense Marketing Strategies' that enable firms to counter Commodity Drift and maintain profitable growth. The first set of strategies -'pro-active' Commodity Drift strategies - attempts to delay Commodity Drift for current market solutions and current target customers. The second set of strategies -'re-active' Commodity Drift strategies -attempts to salvage profitable growth after significant Commodity Drift has already occurred.

Pro-Active Marketing Strategies to Delay Commodity Drift

What can a company do to delay Commodity Drift for its current market solutions and target customers? First, we look at solutions and target customers that are still in the attractive position - the upper-left portion of the Commodity Drift diagram. In this situation, prices and profit margins are still appealing. Forward-looking firms design and implement pro-active strategies to delay the inevitable downward drift toward commoditization.

Think of pro-active strategies like exercising and eating right to stay 'young.' Eventually you will age, and your physical condition will deteriorate, but you can delay that drift by working-out, eating right, and making healthy decisions.

How can we delay the inevitable? Several pro-active strategies can possibly slow Commodity Drift—including the following.

Cut Selective Feature & Service Costs

Identify which current features and services are unvalued or undervalued by the specific target customer, and subsequently cut such services for the target customer in order to reduce costs and increase profit margins.

Raise Prices for Selected Features & Services

Identify features and services that the specific target customer values significantly more than the price currently charged. Then increase the prices and margins for those services, while still leaving a transparent price incentive for the customer.

Innovate with New Features & Services

Use customer feedback, surveys of customers and distributors, and brainstorming to identify brand new, highly-valued, differentiated features and services desired by the target customer. Add those where the customer's perceived value is greater than your costs for providing those features and services. Then you can charge more profitable prices for these new features and services.

Enhance Communications of Highly Valued Features & Services

Enhance the marketing and communications of currently offered features and services that are highly valued by target customers. This helps to maintain higher, more profitable pricing and thus slows Commodity Drift.

Consider these potential pro-active strategies in the context of the Commodity Drift diagram.

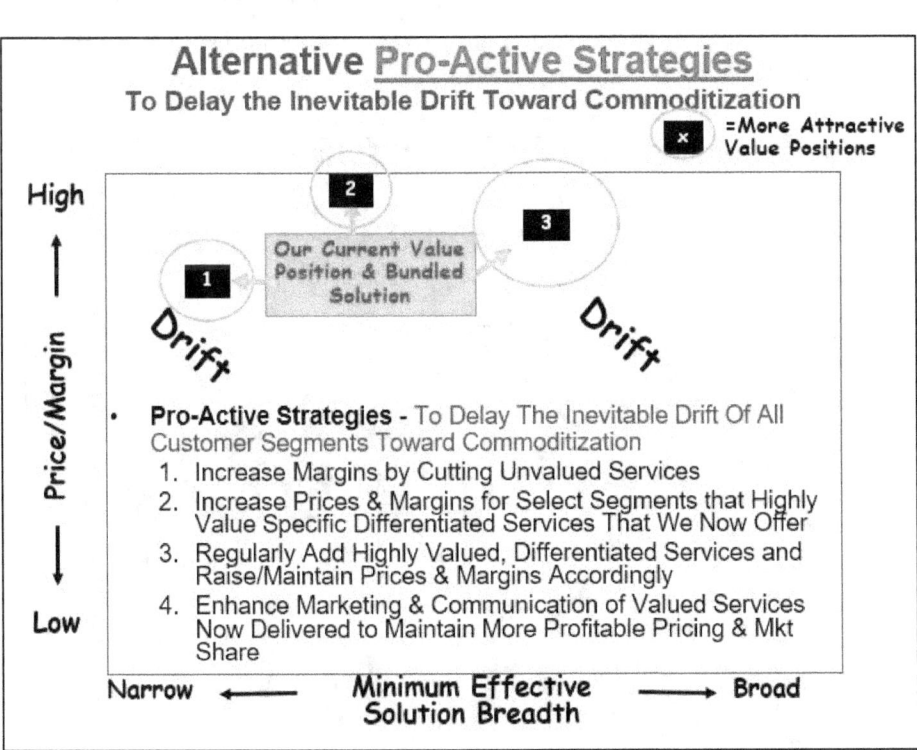

Re-Active Strategies to Counter Commodity Drift that has Already Occurred

Re-active strategies address Commodity Drift that has already occurred. Such strategies seek to rebuild commodity offerings into more valued and customized market solutions for selected target customers. If these re-active strategies prove successful, results can include modest price increases, cost reductions, and enhanced profit margins. The success of these strategies may be short-lived because market deterioration has already occurred, but they represent efforts to make the best of an already bad market situation.

To expand on the health example mentioned earlier, think of re-active Commodity Drift strategies like working-out and eating right to improve significantly-deteriorated health. You have aged and are now at a different stage of life than when you were using pro-active strategies. You search for ways to temporarily reverse or at least slow the continuing downward drift in health by working-out, eating right, etc.

How can you employ a re-active strategy? The re-active strategies nearly duplicate the pro-active strategies, but from a different, much less attractive position on the Commodity Drift grid. The goal of the re-active strategies is to try to slow the downward pressures on profit margins. Re-active Commodity Drift strategies might include any of the following.

Cut Selective Feature & Service Costs

Selectively cut features and services now offered that are unvalued or undervalued by the specific target customers. This will reduce costs and increase profit margins.

Raise Prices for Selected Features & Services

Increase prices and margins for features and services that are still highly valued by the specific target customers, while still leaving a transparent price incentive for the customer and increasing profit margins for the supplier.

Innovate with New Features & Services

Carefully research customers to identify new potential differentiated features and services that would be highly valued by specific target customers. Then add such differentiators – and charge more profitable prices, while promoting these specific new features and services.

Enhance Communications of Highly Valued Features & Services

Enhance the marketing and communications of currently offered features and services that are highly valued by target customers. This will help to maintain higher, more profitable pricing while simultaneously slowing Commodity Drift.

Bailing Out

Finally, bailing out from participation in marketing to certain segments is also an option. Before electing this strategy, however, be sure to assess the potential negative impact (on customers and distributors) of no longer being viewed as a 'full-line' supplier.

Consider these potential re-active strategies in the context of the Commodity Drift diagram.

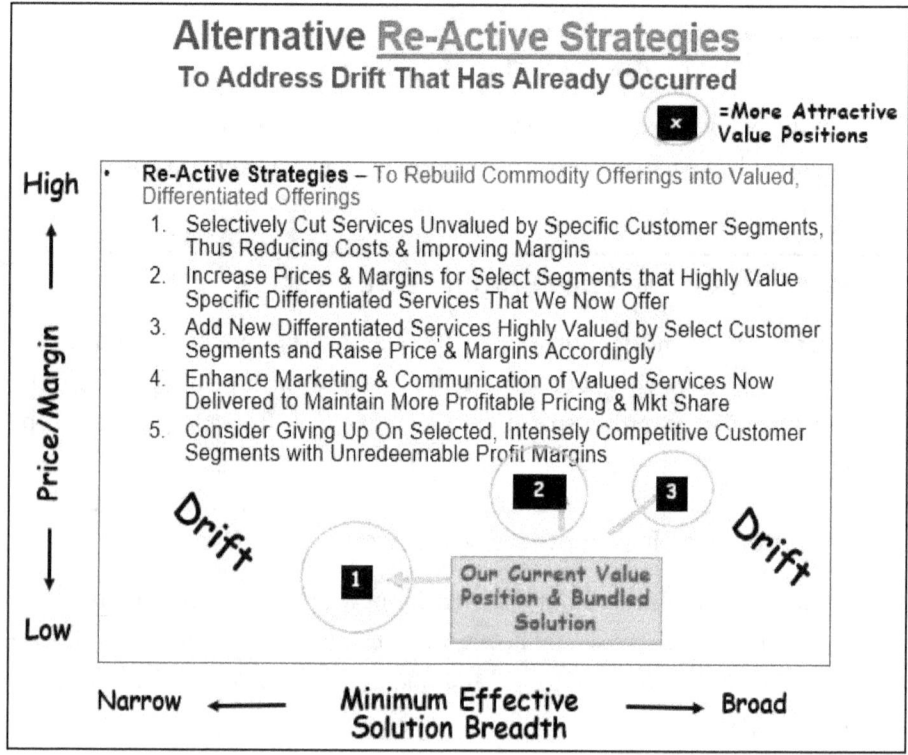

The next growth prerequisite is to **Focus on Value** *(next chapter).*

CHAPTER 6

Focus on Value

In this chapter we continue our discussion on how to achieve steady growth of sales and profits over the long haul.

In the previous chapter we identified strategies for delaying or reversing the price and profit pressures that come with Commodity Drift. A quick referral back to that chapter reveals the *'value focus'* of each potential strategy used to counter Commodity Drift. Given the *value focus* of these strategies, we need to define what *value is and how we can identify which dimensions of our market solution our target customers do indeed 'value.'*

What is Value and How Do We Identify What Target Customers Value? Consider This Scenario.[7]

Customer 'Requirements.

A supplier of closures and terminals for copper and fiber optic cables lost a multimillion dollar customer to a renegade "bare bones" competitor. The customer had been an account for over 15 years and the supplier thought that it completely understood the customer's requirements. When the time came to renew the contract, its sales personnel had visited the customer's plant and asked, 'What would you like from us?' (i.e., what are the Advantages or 'Value Drivers' you want?). The sales personnel came away with a list of detailed product specifications and service requests. In response, the supplier developed and offered a premium-priced "full service" package that it felt would completely meet the customer's stated requirements.

Result

Supplier managers were shocked when they learned that they had lost the account to a new competitor offering a low-priced "no frills" package. Not only did this competitor's offer contain no support services but the products included also fell slightly below the customer's stated specifications. When asked why they had switched to the new vendor, customer managers replied that the competitor's quote was so low, that even if the products failed, the firm would have enough funds available from the cost difference to readily pay for the products to be fixed.

The Lessons of This Scenario

If the sales force spent _more time asking about what specs and services the customer truly valued and was willing to pay for_, then the company could have likely avoided losing this sizable account and could have maybe even increased its profit margins for this account.

For example, the careful query to discover *what this target customer truly valued and was willing to pay for* could have guided the design of each of the Commodity Drift strategies reviewed earlier. More specifically, that exploration could have revealed several opportunities such as the following.

Unvalued Current Services

Are any currently offered services unvalued or undervalued by this target customer? The supplier could subsequently cut such services for this customer, thus reducing costs, and increasing profit margins.

More Highly Valued Current Services

Does the target customer value any currently offered services valued significantly more than the price currently charged for such services? The supplier could increase those prices & margins accordingly, while still leaving a transparent price incentive for the customer.

New Potential Services.

Are there any highly valued, differentiated services desired by, but not yet offered to, the target customer? The supplier could subsequently add those particular new services where the customer's perceived value is greater than the supplier's incremental cost of adding such services - thus providing a higher overall profit margin.

Next Chapter will consider the importance of having "Sustainable Advantages" (Differentiators).

CHAPTER 7

Importance of Having Sustainable Advantages (Differentiators)

In this chapter, we continue discussing various requirements for achieving steady, profitable growth.

There's no faster way to collapse one's profit margins than to haphazardly add new features and services. As seen in the "Adding Unsustainable Advantages" cartoon in this section, rather than slowing Commodity Drift, Kick's has increased the speed of the drift by adding costly features and services, which were then quickly duplicated by Happy Feet, its primary competitor.

Consider Another Example.[8]

Trying to Increase Market Share by Adding New Differentiators.

With a goal of grabbing market in a flat commodity market, a textile producer volunteered to store its products "on consignment" at the plants of a major apparel-producing customer. In addition to keeping the inventory on its own books until used, the textile producer also agreed to:
- Lease warehouse space in the customer's plant to store the inventory
- Furnish an optical scanner and computer system to monitor textile consumption
- Pay for insurance against inventory damage, theft, or loss

Not surprisingly, the customer immediately jumped at the opportunity to implement this innovative program.

Result

What came as a shock to the textile producer was that, within one week, all three of its major competitors had duplicated the program for the apparel producer. Additionally, after a short-term increase in its share of that customer's business, the textile producer saw its market share and those of its competitors return to their preprogram levels. Soon other apparel producers began to demand the same service.

Taking stock at the end of the year, the textile producer discovered that the consignment program had resulted in an overall loss of several million dollars in operating profits. Its managers assumed the same was the case for its competitors. The textile producer took little solace in the fact that its customer satisfaction ratings from the apparel producer had soared to an all-time high.

The Lessons of This Scenario

The lesson from this example is clear. Those who added the new and costly unsustainable advantages were largely responsible for eroding the profits for the entire industry. This occurred because competitors quickly and easily duplicated the costly new features and services added for customers.

After a brief sales spurt, the company adding the unsustainable advantages saw its market share return to its former level. Because competitors were forced to add similar costly features and services, their costs also increased substantially, and profits plummeted across the industry. The various competitors had literally given away previously-attractive profit margins for this industry segment. Customers were obviously delighted!

What New Features & Services Should a Company Add to Stimulate Growth without Compromising Profits?

What new features and services can a company add to stimulate growth without compromising profits? Good question!

First, let's recognize that different market segments typically value the same core solution, but vary in terms of features and services. *Value is the first guideline.* The challenge is to identify which specific features and services are highly valued by each segment. The supplier then pursues ideas for new features and services where its own costs would be substantially less than the true value for the target customer – i.e., less than the price that relevant target customers are willing to pay. Not surprisingly, the supplier discards ideas where its own costs would be greater than the price that its target customers would be willing to pay.

This clearly isn't enough, as shown in the textile example. In that case study, arbitrarily adding even highly valued new features and services had disastrous profit consequences - not only one segment, but for the whole industry! *Sustainability is the second guideline* to use when evaluating which highly valued new features and services one can safely add without compromising segment and industry profits. The key is to add only those unique differentiators that cannot be quickly or easily duplicated by primary competitors.

Potential Sources of Sustainability

Sustainability can come from a variety of sources. For example.

Technological Advantages
- Legally Protected Technology / Patents
- High Complexity and Related Skill Requirement
- Professional Expertise (Number and Quality of Experts)
- Dynamic Technology
- Research and Development (R & D) Budget
- Technology Partnerships and Related Synergistic Benefits

Cost Advantages
- High Initial Investment Requirement
- High Supporting Infrastructure Required
- Operating Cost Efficiency Leader

Scale & Experience Advantages
- Critical Mass / Economy of Scale
- Learning Curve Advantages

Supply Control Advantages
- Control of Critical Supply Source

Market Position Advantage
- Control of Distribution Channels

- Brand Recognition, Image and Loyalty
- Marketing Partnerships and Related Synergistic Benefits
- Superior Customer Relationship Management System

The Bottom Line on Sustainability

The bottom line for the growth planner is this. When attempting to grow sales, market share, and profits through adding new advantages or differentiators, **add only those that are uniquely sustainable – regardless of the source of that sustainability.** Without sustainability, competitors will quickly duplicate any temporarily successful advantages, which will cause both prices and market shares to regress to previous levels. The new costs associated with the added advantages will squeeze profits for all competitors involved. Who wants that? No one - neither you nor your competitors.

CHAPTER 8

Beware of Pricing Traps

Traps you can set for yourself - with a focus on pricing dangers & opportunities for industry leaders

In this chapter, we continue to discuss a series of requirements for achieving steady, profitable growth.

Earlier we examined how Commodity Drift inevitably compresses prices and margins over time. Here we consider some *strategies and related phenomena that can delay the inevitable price and profit crunch, thus contributing to Steady, Profitable Growth!* Such strategies are highly recommended for companies that *can prove* the overall value advantage of their market solution to target customers. In later chapters we will address 'how to prove value advantages.'

Image as a Sustainable Differentiator: The Price Umbrella

Dropping prices is the easiest way to enter a market. Unless aggressive pricing (i.e., lower prices) is based upon unique, sustainable cost advantages, however, it is generally not an attractive growth strategy. If most firms in the relevant industry have similar cost structures, once one competitor begins to make sales and market share inroads through aggressive pricing, others will follow - accelerating the shift in Commodity Drift for all. Any competitor that significantly lowers price without real, sustainable cost advantages can be considered guilty of killing industry-wide profits. That is *not* good marketing!

The Industry Leader Should Provide a Price Umbrella

Well-respected firms that have an image as industry leaders can provide a 'price umbrella' for the industry. Providing a price umbrella means resisting lowering prices in order to help all firms in the industry maintain relatively high profit margins for as long as possible. A leading company can do this without compromising its own sales and market share **because its image as the industry innovator and leader is itself a highly valued, sustainable differentiator** for many target customers.

The price umbrella (i.e., a relatively high price) provided by the leading company or companies reduces the temptation for other competitors to lower their prices and destroy industry profit margins. Thus, a price umbrella provides more time for all competitors to receive higher prices and profit margins. When 'price umbrella leadership' is not present for any specific market solution, the prices and profits are destined to quickly slide down the Commodity Drift drain.

Reaction Threshold

Assume that the primary competitor, Company B, offers a price of $100. Assume also that the industry leader, Company A, can prove to target customers that it has a $20 perceived value advantage over Company B. What price should Company A charge in order to still have a perceived value advantage over Company B?

The logical answer is anything less than $120. But that assumes the customer will shift suppliers whenever there is a perceived value advantage. In the 'real world,' Company A might be able to retain its customers while charging even more than $120. Why? This is because personal and corporate life is difficult enough without re-evaluating brand choices each time one re-buys a product or service. Thus, corporate customers, like regular consumers, establish brand-loyalties to make life simpler by reducing the number of decisions that need to be made each day.

Enter the 'Reaction Threshold.' The reaction threshold is the price at which a company's 'loyal customers' will decide to re-evaluate their brand purchasing habits. Say this threshold for a certain customer is $130 in the example above. If Company A charged $135, the customer might change to Company B's brand and with that change, form a new brand-loyalty. Company A, when realizing it lost that customer, might return with a new offer – say $120, $115, or even less – only to be turned down by that formerly brand-loyal customer. You already know why: as mentioned before, the trouble of re-evaluating brands *yet again* is not worth the potential financial gain.

We bring this up now because when pricing for brand-loyal customers, a company can get a price premium because of the hesitancy of customers to continually re-evaluate their satisfactory brand choices of the past.

Beware of Crossing the Reaction Threshold

The Lesson

A company must know what its brand-loyal customer's 'reaction threshold' is before charging a price higher than the perceived value, before reducing service levels, or before compromising any other dimension of its overall market solution.

CHAPTER 9

Know Your Customers, Your Competitors & Your Market Solution

In this chapter, we continue to discuss a series of requirements for achieving steady, profitable growth.

Know Your Customers and Competitors

It should come as no surprise that companies with more successful growth records are also more committed to regularly monitoring customers and competitors. After all, customers' expectations and competitors' initiatives are the primary forces that drive Commodity Drift.

Successful Companies Monitor the Pulse of Customers and Competitors

45

How the Internet and Social Media have Changed the Game

In the not-too-distant past, before the proliferation of Internet access and social media platforms, many firms were content with casual monitoring of customers and competitors. In fact, as unbelievable as it may seem in today's 'instant information world,' according to a study in the late 1990s, approximately 40% of companies paid little attention to either customers or competitors and fewer than 20% closely monitored both.[9] This lack of external awareness may have been a primary driving force behind the disappointing growth records of many companies during this time.

But that was then, and this is now. The proliferation of Internet access and customers' escalating participation in social media platforms[10] have created new, informed customers. Today, these customers' expectations for nearly all market solutions are becoming more dynamic and demanding each year. And companies had better listen if they want to succeed.

Furthermore, more global competitors are entering the game each year. These are smart players that are *leveraging social media* to succeed in both monitoring and responding to dynamic, heightened customer expectations.

Weak players that do not keep up current trends and have not developed substantive social media strategies to monitor and respond to both dynamic customers' expectations and competitors' offerings are destined to lose their footing on their way down the slippery slope of Commodity Drift.

Know Your *Overall* Market Solution

What could be more important for sales professionals than knowing their overall market solutions inside and out? Nothing, right? If they don't thoroughly understand their solutions, how could anyone to expect them to communicate the value of the solutions to a customer?

Yet ask yourself the following question. *How many times has your company failed to capture a new target customer because your sales folks were not adequately familiar with your overall market solution? Or didn't know what benefits are most highly-valued by the target customer?*

How foolish can a company be in this day and age when the relative value of different features and benefits can change so rapidly, reflecting the ever-more dynamic competition and customer expectations?

This underlines the importance of thorough initial training and periodic re-training to help the sales folks - both new and old - keep up to date with:
- *All the ins and outs of the market solution being offered;*
- *Each market solution's specific values for target customers today; and*
- *Primary competitors' new initiatives in the marketplace.*

This also highlights the importance of having a well-designed, consistent mentoring program for any new person joining the sales team.

CHAPTER 10

Importance of Leadership and Teamwork

In this chapter, we discuss two additional important requirements for achieving steady, profitable growth – Leadership and Teamwork.

Leadership and Teamwork

Most would agree that Peyton Manning and Tom Brady are (or were) outstanding quarterbacks. In fact, they both led their teams, the Colts and Patriots, to the NFL's highest winning percentages (72% and 70%, respectively) during their tenures.

But what if either Manning or Brady had played for the hapless Detroit Lions during that same period – when the Lions won only 26% of their games? Would we still think of him as a great quarterback? Would either have been able to lead the Lions to win 70% of their games? **No way!** Outstanding quarterbacking is much more likely to occur when:
- The quarterback is surrounded by other pro-bowl caliber players;

- The coaching staff develops offensive and defensive schemes that cater to the strengths and weaknesses of individual players; and when
- The coaches and front office draft and make astute trades to address key offensive and defensive player weaknesses.

Yes, 'great quarterbacking' starts with raw talent, but talent alone is not enough to make a great quarterback or 'create a great quarterback image.' That image can only be created when one can successfully leverage initial raw talent with creative and effective teamwork and leadership.

What Does It Take to be a Sales Superstar?

The theme of this Business Growth Secrets 8 Book Series is a company's long-term success depends upon its ability to continually expand the top line sales. Firms that do so invariably have some key 'rain makers,' who set the sales growth bar for the entire sales force. Analogous to a quarterback's raw talent, these top tier sales pros also have basic talent – which typically involves good people skills, magnetic personalities, the drive to succeed, and endless energy to make sales happen. Those qualities alone can enable any sales pro to succeed for a quarter or two and maybe a bit longer. But those qualities are *not enough* to ensure long-term selling success for any would-be sales superstar.

Sales pros who are top performers *year after year* leverage natural selling talents with several other critical characteristics. **<u>First, they are prepared</u>**. As considered earlier, they continually monitor dynamic customer needs and expectations as well as strategic initiatives of primary competitors. They also keep themselves right up to date on all features and services of each of the different market solutions they may be selling.

Who's He?

Each of the following quarterbacks had solid raw talent, but no one considers them to have been great NFL quarterbacks.

Joey Harrington #3 overall draft pick (Detroit Lions) in 2002. Who's he? Lions won only 26% of their games between 2000 and 2010.[11]

Tim Couch #1 overall draft pick (Cleveland Browns) in 1999. Who's he? Browns won only 36% of their games between 2000 and 2010.

David Carr #1 overall draft pick (Houston Texans) in 2002. Who's he? Texans won only 38% of their games between 2000 and 2010.

<u>JOEY HARRINGTON</u>   <u>TIM COUCH</u>   <u>DAVID CARR</u>

But there's more! Top sales pros **<u>also have enlightened leaders</u>**, who know the dangers of static market solutions in dynamic markets. Such leaders provide vibrant market solutions that respond to both ever-changing customer expectations and to evermore threatening competitive initiatives. Successful sales pros *also* **<u>team with company experts</u>** whose jobs include monitoring the pulse of target customers and primary competitors.

Star 'Rainmakers' Are Made, Not Born

Different members of the sales team possess varying levels of natural selling talent.

Can a sales pro with non-optimal natural selling skills turn into a sales superstar? You bet! In fact, some of your own key rainmakers have likely done just that, by successfully overlaying sometimes mediocre natural selling skills with a commitment to superior performance in:

- Keeping up to date on dynamic customer needs and expectations as well as strategic initiatives of primary competitors;
- Keeping up to date on all features and services of each of the different market solutions they may be selling;
- Working closely with leaders in providing advice to help in the development of dynamic market solutions that respond to ever-changing customers and competitive initiatives;
- Teaming with company experts whose jobs include monitoring the pulse of target customers and primary competitors; *and* by
- Becoming intimately familiar with and methodically following the company's single selling 'system.'

Sales Superstars Leverage Social Media

Your most productive sales professionals today most certainly work very closely with your social media team members, who monitor the pulse of target customers and primary competitors more and more effectively each year. This collaboration enables the most effective sales pros to leverage information flowing from a variety of social media sources in order to enhance their selling performance.

For example, monitoring social media enables them to:
- Obtain more accurate and timely information on dynamic customer needs and expectations as well as on strategic initiatives of primary competitors;
- Follow customer demands and concerns (expressed in interest groups) more closely in order to keep right up-to-date on dynamic customer demands for new features and services for your self-checkout systems; and to
- Become aware of dynamic customer and competitor market patterns and subsequently relay more accurate and timely information on these patterns to your product development, IT, and customer service and support groups.

CHAPTER 11

A 'Master Selling Approach' Drives Growth

In this chapter, we discuss the final requirement for achieving steady, profitable growth – a **'Master Selling Approach.'**

Let's Change Gears for a Moment

As emphasized earlier, Commodity Drift will ultimately destroy the profits for every single solution and segment over time. That's a challenging backdrop for any company hoping for steady, long-term, profitable growth! It is a challenge that requires regularly attacking the marketplace with new solutions, new uses for old solutions, and new segments for both old and new solutions. So that's our starting point: "Any company hoping for steady profitable growth needs to continually pursue new opportunities (solutions, uses, or segments)." Now where do we go from here?

Consider This

If Company A and Company B are both continually pursuing new opportunities, as required by unavoidable Commodity Drift, <u>then, how can Company A continually outperform Company B when it comes to the bottom line – i.e., achieving steady, long-term profitable growth?</u>

What's the Secret?

The 'secret' is this: <u>**Company A is winning because its sales professionals are much better at capturing the individual sale**</u> – *i.e., winning the deal. This variation in the 'close ratios' of the sales forces of the two companies is* <u>**unrelated to**</u> *which particular innovative solutions are introduced and which new segments are being attacked.*

Really?? Yes, Really! *Here's how we're going to try to explain this. We are going to show you one well thought-out selling process.* We will explain how consistently and effectively using a single, solid selling process or 'system' will enable sales pros at Company A to consistently outperform their sales pro counterparts at Company B.

We are not suggesting a 'magic selling elixir' - because, as we all know, there is no fool-proof selling process. In fact, **there are dozens of different, solid selling processes** that are helping firms around the globe to achieve steady, profitable sales growth. Just a few of the more popular selling 'systems' (you've likely heard of many if not most of these) include: Holden International (Power Base Selling), Huthwaite (Spin Selling), Miller Heiman (Conceptual Selling), On Target / BRS (Target Account Selling), Sales Performance International (SPI) (Solution Selling®), and Selling Communications (Target Selling).

A 'Master Selling Approach' Drives the Growth Plan

So, what are we suggesting? The point is this: Company A is more successful than Company B because it invested in and has perfected one single selling process for its entire sales team. The whole team understands and uses the same process. The process has been refined and adapted for the specific solutions that Company A sells. The whole sales team contributes to refining the system over time and participates regularly in training themselves and new members of the sales team on all dimensions of the system.

The Whole Sales Team Should Use the Same Selling Approach

How the Sales Team Benefits from Using a Single, Solid Selling Approach

Using a single, detailed selling process – regardless of which specific system is used - has multiple benefits. Consider how using a single, well-designed selling process or method benefits the whole sales force:

Benefits of a Single Process for All

The *first set of benefits* focuses on *achieving improved close ratios on individual accounts for the whole sales team* by:

- **Enabling** *sales rookies* (with considerable live mentoring) **to hit the ground running;**
- **Helping** *grizzled old veterans* **to enhance their sales performance, once they can be convinced to buy into the system** (sometimes a challenging task!);
- **Helping** *solid sales force performers* **become super performers; and**
- **Helping those who are already** *sales superstars* **to generate even better sales and profit growth numbers.**

How the Sales & Marketing Management Team Also Benefit from a Single Selling Approach

A critical *second set of benefits* answers the prayers of sales supervisors, such as Sales Managers, Sales Directors, VPs of Sales, Marketing Directors, Marketing Managers, and the VP of Marketing or CMO.

Benefits of a Single Process for Sales & Marketing Managers

- The <u>*second set of benefits*</u> answers the prayers of sales supervisors, such as Sales Managers, Sales Directors, VPs of Sales, Marketing Directors, Marketing Managers, and the VP of Marketing or CMO.
- **Reaping the relevant benefits for these types of sales supervisors depends upon:**
  - A rigid commitment to the same *exact* selling process by the entire sales force;
  - Overlaying the process with technology-enabled live reports from sales folks in the field [which provide timely updates on progress made (or not made) on every single important sales effort underway.]

Benefits for Sales & Marketing Managers, cont.

- *Sales supervisors* **at all levels now have potential quantitative bases for:**
  - More accurately projecting operating period results *during each operating period* – rather than awaiting unpredictable numbers at the end of the quarter;
  - Stepping in with *coaching aids during the quarter* to help individual sales folks stuck in any step of the selling process with important prospective clients;
  - Knowing ahead of time when the 'sales hopper' is getting thin at any place – top to bottom – and stepping in to *generate more new prospects* (via new solutions, new uses, new target segments, or simply more innovative and aggressive prospecting) as well as to stimulate selective sales efforts already underway.

Implemented properly, this can ensure steady, long-term, profitable sales growth for the company – the goal of the Business Growth Secrets book series.

Now, What's Next?

So, we see that steady, long-term, profitable growth is driven by a 'Master Selling Approach' for each individual account. Let's repeat that - *steady, long-term, profitable growth is driven by a 'Master Selling Approach' for each individual account.* That is a critical point, as it frames the entire growth planning process that is detailed in the rest of this Business Growth Secrets book series!

Most of the latter books in this series focus on the "how to" for capturing the individual sale – for that skill is what will ultimately drive revenue & profit growth. That is, a company cannot expect to grow unless its sales team can consistently turn target customers into actual customers.

After we present the details of one particular selling system (applying it in a single case study), we'll return in the latter books of the Business Growth Secrets book series to emphasize and explain how ongoing, singular sales efforts and successes fit into a larger framework that overlays marketing and sales. Such an over-encompassing framework, properly designed, implemented and utilized *can virtually ensure continuous company success in profitably selling to customer after customer.*

The remaining books in the series detail how any company can significantly improve its close ratios for capturing individual sale after sale – and then translating that into continuous, aggressive sales and profit growth. These logically integrated follow-on books include:

> Book 2: Secrets to Planning Sales Growth
> Book 3: Secrets to Preparing for Sales Growth, Part 1
> Book 4: Secrets to Preparing for Sales Growth, Part 2
> Book 5: *Secrets to Making the Sale, Part 1*
> Book 6: *Secrets to Making the Sale, Part 2*
> Book 7: Secrets to Negotiating, Closing & Implementation
> Book 8: Secrets to Ensuring Continuous Sales Growth

The specific selling system a company chooses does not matter. *A good sales professional can succeed over the long-term using virtually any well thought out systematic selling process.* The general outline of SPI's "Solution Selling®" system[12] is favored in this book because it is practical, logical, and easily adapted to a broad array of market solutions and segments.

Notes

1 Spencer Stuart Study 2006 - cited in Fast Company, 6/07
2 Francis Goh, "10 Companies that Failed to Innovate Resulting in Business Failure" https://www.collectivecampus.io/blog/10-companies-that-were-too-slow-to-respond-to-change
3 Ibid.
4 https://money.cnn.com/2011/11/10/pf/walmart_black_friday/index.htm
5 Adapted from Anderson, J., and J. Narus, Business Market Management, Prentice Hall, (1st Edition).
6 While a variation is presented here, the Commodity Drift concept flows from: V. K. Rangan and G.T Bowman, "Beating the Commodity Magnet," Industrial Marketing Management, 21: 215-222.
7 Anderson, J., and J. Narus. Business Market Management: Understanding, Creating and Delivering Value. (1st edition), Prentice Hall.
8 Anderson, J., and J. Narus. Business Market Management: Understanding, Creating and Delivering Value. (1st edition), Prentice Hall.
9 Weber, John A., "Illusions of Marketing Planners," Psychology and Marketing, Vol. 18, no. 6, 527-563.
10 Refer to later chapter on Social Marketing Strategies
11 In deference to the too oft frustrated 'Lion faithful,' it is certainly possible, but remains to be seen, whether Mathew Stafford, the #1 overall pick by Detroit in 2009, will become a 'great quarterback.' This will depend upon the performance of other high draft picks by the Detroit in more recent years, the effectiveness of the revolving coaching team, and the extent to which the Lion's improve their win percentage over the years.
12 The Solution Selling® terminology and constructs presented in this book come from Sales Performance International (SPI - http://www.spisales.com/ - Charlotte, NC). See Keith Eades, The New Solution Selling®, McGraw Hill. Dr. Weber is a certified instructor of Solution Selling®. This Business Growth Secrets series presents his interpretation & expansion of the Solution Selling® system, without SPI's carte blanche endorsement of the specifics of that interpretation & expansion.

www.ingramcontent.com/pod-product-compliance
Lightning Source LLC
Chambersburg PA
CBHW071147240526
45465CB00024BA/1808